T0198977

Heaven...More Than We Can Dream

A Book for People of All Ages

Kathleen M. McGuire

WestBow Press books may be ordered through booksellers or by contacting:

WestBow Press
A Division of Thomas Nelson & Zondervan
1663 Liberty Drive
Bloomington, IN 47403
www.westbowpress.com
1 (866) 928-1240

NASB: Scripture quotations taken from the New American Standard Bible® (NASB), Copyright © 1960, 1962, 1963, 1968, 1971, 1972, 1973, 1975, 1977, 1995 by The Lockman Foundation Used by permission. www.Lockman.org

ISBN: 978-1-9736-7456-6 (sc)
ISBN: 978-1-9736-7457-3 (e)

Library of Congress Control Number: 2019913750

Print information available on the last page.

WestBow Press rev. date: 09/24/2019

WESTBOW
P R E S S®
A DIVISION OF THOMAS NELSON
& ZONDERVAN

Dedication

━━━◆❈◆━━━

This book is dedicated to Rita Ronning (3/20/51-5/23/19). We had many deaths this year in the community where I live; however, Rita's impacted me the most. I hardly knew her but she was relatively young and her death was totally unexpected. It triggered all the thoughts about...ya never know how much time we have here on earth, etc., etc.. So shortly after her death, I was at our dog park, at sunrise, just myself and my dog and I was thinking about Rita and our limited time. I have known for about 30 years that God has wanted me to write poetry for Him but I've written very few in all those years. Then my spirit said, "If you're gonna write for God, there's no time like the present to start!" And I wrote the first few verses of this book right then and there!

Acknowledgement

I'd like to give a special thanks to my bible study group, friends and family for their continued support, prayers and encouragement.

I've always wondered
  is heaven for real...
what is it like?

Is it all I've ever
  dreamed of...
a blessed delight?

Will we be like angels
        floating on clouds...
like in stories and all?

Is it really up in the
        clouds somewhere;
Is it big or small?

Is it as beautiful as
    palm trees,
glistening in the sun?

Swaying and dancing
    in the wind...
just having fun?!

Or like the most
	spectacular sunset
that you've ever seen?

With orange, pinks and reds
	dropping into the ocean
or so it seems?

Will we see our friends,
  family and pets
that went on before us?

Will we get to meet God
  face to face
and sit with Jesus?

What music will we hear
in heaven?
LeAnn Rime's "Blue"?

After all I have
heard it said that
God loves "country" too!

And what will our food
        intake consist of...
things that aren't good for you?

Like chocolate candy, pies
        and cakes galore...
and ice cream too?!

AL DiMAURO

Well, no not exactly so
  I hear tell,
but heaven is for real.

It's beyond our wildest
  imagination...
totally surreal.

Now listen to what I
  have to tell,
it will seem quite extreme.

But it's God's picture of what
  heaven is like...
it's more than we can dream!

God tells us it is a very
    huge place
with many, many rooms.[1]

We will have plenty to eat
    from fruit trees
that monthly have blooms.[2,3]

And I'm sure the angels
    song will surpass
the best we've ever heard.

Numbering ten thousands upon
    ten thousands,[4]
singing like a bird.

There will be a river of
        life through it
and streets of pure gold!

And the gates will be a
        single pearl...
hard to behold![5]

The foundation will be made
    of brilliant gems...
rubies and agates, too!

Amethists, emeralds and
    jasper...Wow!
Just to name a few![6]

There will be no light from
    the sun or moon...
so how will we see?

The glory of God will shine
    on us all;
daytime will go on endlessly![7,8]

There will be no worry,
       guilt or sin;
mainly just pure love.

No illnesses or
       disabilities...
all healed from above.[9]

The best part is meeting
     God and Jesus...
that's a fact!

We'll get to walk with them
     and talk with them....
can you imagine that!?!

How do I know all this
    is true, you ask...
the bible tells me so.

And I'm not arguing
    with that word...
absolutely no!

So when I die, don't
        be sad and blue...
please be happy for me.

Because I will have
        graduated
into heavenly glee!

Endnotes

1 John 14:2...“In My Father's house are many dwelling places; if it were not so, I would have told you; for I go to prepare a place for you.”

2 *Ezekiel 47:12...“And by the river on its bank, on one side and on the other, will grow all kinds of trees for food. Their leaves will not wither, and their fruit will not fail. They will bear every month because their water flows from the sanctuary, and their fruit will be for food and their leaves for healing.”*

3 Revelation 22:2...And on either side of the river was the tree of life, bearing twelve kinds of fruit, yielding its fruit every month; and the leaves of the tree were for healing of the nations.

4 Revelation 5:11...And I looked, and I heard the voices of many angels around the throne and the living creatures and the elders; and the number of them was myriads of myriads, and thousands of thousands.

5 Revelation 21:21...And the twelve gates were twelve pearls; each one of the gates was a single pearl. And the street of the city was pure gold, like transparent glass.

6 Revelation 21:18-20...18 And the material of the wall was jasper; and the city was pure gold, like clear glass. 19 The foundation stones of the city wall were adorned with every kind of precious stone. The first foundation stone was jasper; the second, sapphire; the third, chalcedony; the fourth, emerald; 20 the fifth, sardonyx; the sixth, sardius; the seventh, chrysolite; the eight, beryl; the ninth, topaz; the tenth, chrysoprase; the eleventh, jacinth; the twelfth, amethyst.

7 Revelation 21:23 & 25...23 And the city has no need of the sun or of the moon to shine upon it, for the glory of God has illuminated it, and its lamp is the lamb. 25 And in the daytime (for there shall be no night there) its gates shall never be closed;...

8 Revelation 22:5...And there shall no longer be any night; and they shall not have need of the light of a lamp nor the light of the sun, because the Lord God shall illuminate them; and they shall reign forever and ever.

9 Revelation 21:4...And He shall wipe away every tear from their eyes; and there shall no longer be any death; there shall no longer be any mourning or crying or pain; the first things have passed away.

About the illustrator

---◆—╳—◆---

Al DiMauro has been an artist for many decades. His artwork
is displayed all over the world. His art reflects the glory of God.

About the author

Kathleen (Kathy) McGuire has been a Christian for 35 years but just recently the vision of heaven became real for her. Sure, she'd read Revelation early on when she first became a born again Christian. However, over the years what she has read about heaven became distant in her mind and therefore, was like a fantasy. It wasn't until Kathy was leading a study on heaven with a small bible study group in her community that re-reading parts of Revelation actually became a revelation for her! Even though Kathy was leading the study, she thinks she was probably the most impacted. Knowing that the bible is God's word and therefore is truth, made her realize what heaven really will be like. So out of her heart came this poem and subsequent book. It is Kathy's hope and prayer that the words and beautiful illustrations on the pages of this book will help you to also visualize heaven as reality.